40 Common Errors
IN SOCCER
and How to Correct Them

Photograph by Alan Tepp

40 Common Errors
IN SOCCER
and How to Correct Them

Arthur Shay
with
Coach Ed Kositzki

Contemporary Books, Inc.
Chicago

Library of Congress Cataloging in Publication Data

Shay, Arthur.
    40 Common errors in soccer and how to correct them.

    Includes index.
    1. Soccer.   2. Soccer—Coaching.   I. Kositzki, Ed,
joint author.   II. Title.
GV943.S46   1979   796.33'42   78-73675
ISBN 0-8092-7322-5
ISBN 0-8092-7321-7 pbk.

Published by Contemporary Books, Inc.
180 North Michigan Avenue, Chicago, Illinois 60601
Manufactured in the United States of America
Library of Congress Catalog Card Number: 78-73675
International Standard Book Number: 0-8092-7322-5 (cloth)
                                    0-8092-7321-7 (paper)

Published simultaneously in Canada by
Beaverbooks
953 Dillingham Road
Pickering, Ontario L1W 1Z7
Canada

This book is for my friends Sam and Denyse Grode, who, like soccer, came here from a distant country and made our country a better place by their coming.

Contents

Acknowledgments

Thanks to players Phillip Shively, George Hoffman, Todd Steckbeck, and Dave Rutledge for demonstrating various mistakes and corrections.

Special thanks to Robert Metcalf, Superintendent of Community High School District 115, Lake Forest, Illinois, for the use of Lake Forest High School's six beautiful soccer fields, and to Lake Forest coach Ed Kositzki for his suggestions.

Thanks to my son, reporter-photographer Steve Shay, for his assistance, and to Lee Stern, owner of the Chicago Sting, for his encouragement.

Introduction

The most popular sport in the world is soccer. More people follow the ups and downs of soccer teams in 150 countries than follow the fortunes of any other team sport. The awarding of the International World's Cup, sponsored by FIFA (Federation Internationale Football Association), the world governing body of soccer, is a time of madness, riot, suicide, but mostly joy. The hardy practitioners of the sport regularly draw a billion TV viewers. More importantly, they have inspired what was first a ground swell but is now a worldwide soccer boom amongst the young. Happily, at long last, soccer has begun to come into its own in the United States. More than six thousand high schools and eight hundred colleges now have teams. Women's teams are on the rise, as are leagues in which boys and girls of all ages compete regularly. Nearly a million pre-high school boys and girls belong to the American Youth Soccer Organization.

Sponsoring industries, such as Coca-Cola, are helping school and club teams secure good equipment. The U.S. Soccer Federation, the North American Soccer League and several new organizations promoting indoor, off-season soccer are beginning to flourish.

It was about a hundred years ago that soccer branched off from rugby, and rugby became American football. In the interim, ethnic, school, and finally professional league teams have brought the sport into full and privileged status as both a spectator and participant sport.

Such early aficionados as Chicago Sting owner Lee Stern have invested heavily in soccer's popularity in this country. "My coaches go to Europe and South America to look for players," Stern told a reporter recently. "But with soccer booming at the school level in the U.S., we're also scouting lots of good high school and college teams."

One of the teams that Stern watches carefully is the one at Lake Forest High School near Chicago which is coached by a former Northern Illinois University collegiate star and All-American, Ed Kositzki, who often works out with The Sting and is assistant director of their summer soccer camps.

After speaking with several soccer coaches I asked Ed Kositzki if my son and assistant Steve Shay and I could follow him around with cameras and notebooks and watch him correct the common errors that aspiring soccer players make.

At first Ed Kositzki was a little self-conscious about coaching his team members to make mistakes. But in a little while he became completely immersed in dividing his favorite sport into its relatively uncomplicated components and examining each of them.

"Some of these players will be playing for college teams," says Kositzki proudly, "and after that will probably be the first generation of completely homegrown soccer pros."

Whether or not your youngster wants to become a big leaguer in the traditional baseball or football American dream, we hope that this book will help him or her develop a good foundation in the sport.

Arthur Shay

Chapter 1
Equipment and warm-up

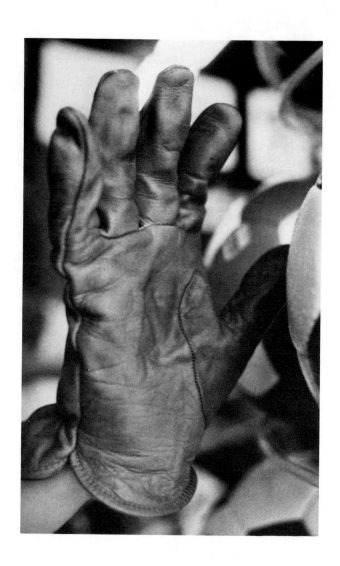

MISTAKE

Bad equipment

Like most sports, soccer is a game of inches. Defeat or victory hangs on trifling distances, differences, moments—and advantages and disadvantages of equipment.

Cheap shoes that don't fit snugly enough can take their toll on the field causing injuries and losses without even seeming to be the culprits.

Shorts that are too tight can make a player just uncomfortable enough to miss a crucial shot or save. Socks that creep fall in this category too.

Ordinary driving or skiing gloves used by a goalie can easily let a hard kicked slippery ball slither in for a goal.

2

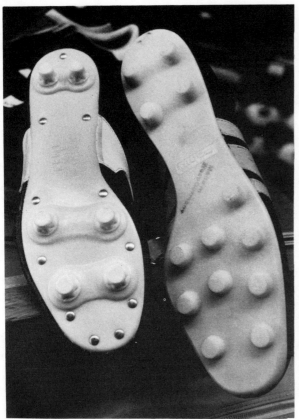

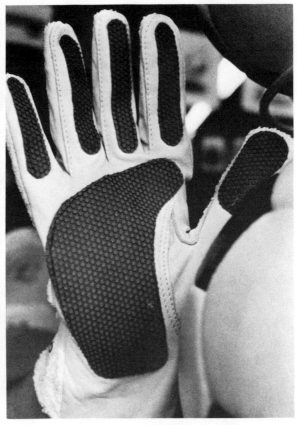

CORRECTION

Shoes are of primary importance in soccer. Lightweight leather boots are made by most shoe companies supplying soccer boots worldwide. Protective padding smoothly tooled into the arch, heel, and around the edges help protect the feet and help what Pele calls his "good old friends" carry the player through many a game. Molded studs in the soles are most popular and effective for hard earth and synthetic fields. Screw-in studs are used at the coach's discretion, for wet-ground play, *but never on synthetic turf.* Spare pairs of playing shoes and practice sneakers are a good idea. Sweat-absorbing cotton-rayon shirts are more popular these days than nylon. The best socks are those that can stay up without elastic bands. Goalie gloves with tiny suction cups attached are available, legal, and effective.

3

MISTAKE

Running without the ball

Running is the basic conditioning exercise for soccer. But the soccer ball is the reason for the running. Simple jogging without a soccer ball wastes ball-handling time and energy that could be better spent.

CORRECTION

A few slow laps around the field while kicking the ball in short, zigzag patterns, helps the beginning soccer player develop the kind of running skill that combines with foot and eye coordination, and helps form a complete player. This is called functional practice. Functional practice involves the ball in as many combinations as possible. The ball should become an imagined extension of the would-be player. It is from this kind of practice that proficient ball control comes.

MISTAKE

Sit-ups without ball

The sit-up is the basic waistline exercise in soccer as it is in most sports. Doing sit-ups without the ball deprives the soccer student of ball-consciousness that the natural player either has or develops.

6

CORRECTION

The joke in this exercise, of course, is that this is one of the few times a soccer player can touch the ball. Rolling the ball to the left, the right and the center in sets of two improves muscle tone, develops flexibility and helps keep the mind on the ball! Twenty-five repetitions each session is recommended.

Dettmar Creamer of the German National Team is generally acknowledged to have started this kind of practice that Coach Ed Kositzki and many others use in training young soccer players.

7

MISTAKE

Starting with scrimmage

Eager newcomers to soccer are so anxious to start playing they often neglect to warm up properly. Poor warm-up can result in injury to suddenly stretched muscles. It also results in poor soccer, because the reflexes need a few minutes of preparation.

8

CORRECTION

Using the soccer ball as a prop, a new player should do at least five minutes of stretching exercises before any scrimmage. The ball should be passed rhythmically through the legs and around the legs with the waist rocking each time.

Soccer combines much of the grace of good dancing. A good beginning exercise is a series of alternating jump steps in which the toe just touches the ball. Left toe, jump, right toe, etc. Kind of a rope skipping step.

Jumping over the ball, left and right, develops stamina, leg and ankle strength, and that all-important ball sense vital to soccer. Moreover, it teaches the player to concentrate and focus on the soccer problem of the moment. A good warm-up helps the soccer player achieve playing-readiness—a perfect combination of physical and mental preparedness.

Chapter 2
Ball and body control

MISTAKE

Pointed toe

There is a strong temptation on the part of beginning players to use the point of the toe as the striking area of the foot against the ball. This minimizes the power the foot is capable of transmitting to the ball, and works against pinpoint accuracy in shooting or passing.

CORRECTION

The instep is the most common striking surface of the foot on the soccer ball. However the outside of the foot is also a valuable weapon in passing and in deceiving an opponent. As your proficiency in soccer increases, you will be able to use the inside and outside kicking areas to curve the ball towards a teammate or away from a defender, and, best of all, out of the clutches of a goalie.

MISTAKE

Leaning

New soccer players just beginning to feel control of the ball often lapse into the bad habit of leaning backward to achieve some kind of meeting between foot and ball. The trouble is that when the body leans way back, or even part of the way back, it loses a good part of its function as the power and coiled-spring base of a good kick. It also works to keep your eyes off the ball. This position, furthermore, leaves you vulnerable to a sure-footed intercepter.

CORRECTION

The body works best for kicking a soccer ball when it is just about over the ball, with the standing (non-kicking) foot next to the ball. All the lean should come forward as your body's power is imparted to the ball through your kicking foot.

MISTAKE

Clowning

Most soccer injuries during practice result from clowning around! The ball starts flying around; wild kicks find unexpected targets on parts of the body. The game of soccer is reduced to child's play.

16

CORRECTION

If you are lucky enough to have a wall with a painted or chalked in goal, use it to refine your shots, not as an immovable background for horseplay!

Line your practice balls up at various distances from your target goal, and take turns at shooting or even passing.

Orderly practice and procedure will add to your knowledge and appreciation of soccer and prevent easily avoidable injuries due to clowning.

MISTAKE

Trapping yourself

Using the body to trap the ball is an important move in soccer. The trouble comes when the player is so thrilled with his trap that he neglects to move the ball into the vital next stage and the ball just sits there in front of him.

CORRECTION

Modern soccer is fluid, not static. One move leads into the next. Trapping the ball on one side of your chest will often give you a moment's jump on your opponent or can spell the difference between retaining possession of the ball or losing it.

The trapped ball should be moved instantaneously to head or foot as part of a sequence that is aimed at moving the ball goalward.

For some reason women players seem to accomplish trapping as part of an on-going sequence better than male players.

19

MISTAKE

Mid-air disaster

The ball comes at you in mid-air, higher than you'd like. Your kicking foot lashes out wildly and too often at too wide an angle to make up for the unfamiliar trajectory.

CORRECTION

Even in the air, your kicking foot should strike the ball the same way it would perform on a ground shot. The knee should be up and out, heel down, toes up, and the inside of the foot contacting the ball.

MISTAKE

Heading for trouble

Soccer is one of the few sports in which the head is used as a physical force. In actual practice, as a striking tool, many soccer games are lost because the player striking the ball with his head has not really used his head to best advantage.

The strongest bone in the human body, physiologists tell us, is the forehead bone. It was designed so strongly because of its main function—protecting the brain! It is the head's best ball-striking area.

Many of the heading errors in soccer come when the player closes his eyes just before contact with the ball resulting in a blow to the nose or mouth.

Other, rounder parts of the head than the forehead are sometimes used but they are not, in practice, reliable.

CORRECTION

That wonderfully strong, flat forehead between eyebrows and scalp should be used to head the ball goalwards, forward, or to another teammate.

For well-timed head shots of good distance, the entire body must act like a coiled spring—stomach muscles, back muscles, knees, thighs, and neck muscles working together.

With those crucial eyes open, the body must be uncoiled and thrust at that ball. This is called jump heading.

Stationary heading is accomplished with the feet in place and the rest of the body providing the coiling motion that is, at the moment of striking, imparted to the ball.

MISTAKE

Using hand to start juggling

Juggling the ball—keeping it in the air by using your feet, thighs, head and chest—should never be started, as the player in the background is demonstrating, using your hands! The most important rule of soccer is that, except for the goalie, the hands are a no-no! Using the hands in even so simple a maneuver as starting to juggle the ball keeps the body from learning to function without those hands!

CORRECTION

The feet are entirely capable of getting the ball into the air for a good warm-up, juggling drill. The student should practice this drill in twos: Juggle twice with each foot, twice with the head, twice with the thigh, and so on. The natural inclination of the beginner to use the hands as aids must be overcome in these drills.

MISTAKE

Not using your body

Soccer is so foot and head oriented, the rest of your body is often ignored. When an opponent bent on stealing (tackling) that precious ball comes in for his attack it's a mistake to depend on your legs alone. If he has built up some momentum and is well focused he can overcome your footwork.

26

CORRECTION

You must protect your ball by trying to dribble with the foot that's further away from your opponent. You must then use your body to shield or screen the ball from your opponent and move inside his attempted steal, leaving him looking at your back if possible.

27

Chapter 3
Dribbling

MISTAKE

Dribble chasing

It is easy to misuse the basic soccer maneuver of dribbling the ball in the direction of the enemy goal by letting the ball get too far ahead of you. The resulting loss of control makes it easy for an opponent to intercept the ball.

CORRECTION

The basic dribble is really a series of gentle, controlled pushes. The soccer beginner should think "push," not "kick." The dribbled ball should be pushed in front of you with short thrusts. When the time to kick, shoot for a goal or pass comes, the "pushed" ball is a lot easier to manage than a ball that must be chased and recaptured by the dribbler.

31

MISTAKE

Losing the ball while dribbling

If you persist on letting the ball get too far ahead of you in dribbling during a game and compound it by trying to fake your way around your opponent, he will easily be able to beat you to the ball if it comes anywhere near him.

CORRECTION

The best method to beat an opponent in a dribble is to approach him with the ball close to your better dribbling foot—*as close as one stride from him!* Fake him out with a tap to that side when he moves to tackle* the ball (steal it from you). Then quickly bring it back to the other side, accelerating quickly past him. At this point you must be alert for your next maneuver which could be a pass to a teammate or a shot at the goal.

---

*In soccer, tackling means gaining possession of the ball from an opponent. You don't "tackle" a player as in football. In soccer you "tackle" the ball, never the player.

MISTAKE

Overrunning the ball

The second most common dribbling error is letting the ball lag so slowly that you overrun it, sometimes tripping yourself on it. The difficulty here is that the player out-runs the ball. That is, runs past it. Obviously, you can't control the ball when you've out-run it.

34

CORRECTION

With the ball in control just in front of you, you should practice controlling it by changing its direction. Generally it's best to move the ball to the left with the inside of the kicking foot and to the right with the outside of the foot.

Chapter 4

Passing

MISTAKE

Kick-passing

Passing is one of the principal methods of advancing the ball towards the opposition goal. If you get in the habit of "just kicking" the ball ahead instead of kicking it to a teammate, or to a spot where he'll be in a moment, you will help defeat yourself and your team.

CORRECTION

The name of the game is to keep those passes away from those enemy jerseys! This is best done by passing to friendly jerseys. You must allow for an opponent's speed and momentum, and keep the ball out of his reach while angling it towards the teammate in the best position to receive your pass, and move the ball downfield towards the goal.

MISTAKE

Crooked passing

You have fairly good control of the ball.
Your opponent is moving in. Your teammate is in a good position to receive your
pass. Your kicking leg heaves back but
the ball angles away on a crooked path
and is scooped up by the enemy.

40

CORRECTION

Correcting the crooked pass involves having the standing (non-kicking) foot aim at the proposed line of flight of the ball. The heel of the kicking foot is down, the toes are pointing slightly upwards. The kicking knee is pointed out and the ball is struck smoothly with the side of the foot, making a reasonably square surface hitting that ball. The ball should then roll along the ground on its intended path to your teammate.

41

MISTAKE

High for low, low for high

The most frustrating part of learning soccer is kicking the ball and having it go anyplace but where you want it to go. As common as the crooked pass are errors in height and roll. You want the ball to go like a chip shot with just a little arc, up and over an opponent, but instead it rolls straight. You want to roll that ball straight to a teammate and you execute a perfect but unwanted "chip."

CORRECTION

To roll the ball, you must meet the center of the ball with the center of your instep. Generally this means raising your kicking leg slightly.

MISTAKE

Hanging back

When receiving a pass from a teammate, don't wait for the ball to come to you. If you do, you risk interception and other problems stemming from the increased time that the ball is en route. (Among the "other problems" is a slowing down of initiative and forward thrust, even team spirit.)

44

CORRECTION

The rule of thumb is: always move towards the ball, capturing it as soon as possible so as to pass it along, shoot it, or do whatever is necessary to improve your team's position. You should use your body to shield the ball from a defender, turning your back to him when possible, forcing him to catch up with you and come around you if he wants to get the ball you have just received.

MISTAKE

Poor timing

A give and go pass is the most common and effective pass in soccer except when either the "give" or the "go" pass is intercepted by a defender!

If the pass is made too soon, as in this case, the defensive player can easily intercept. Passing too late has obviously related problems.

CORRECTION

The ideal is to pass at the right time. In this sequence the attacker waited until the defender was quite close and had committed himself to a tackle. Then he passed, cut downfield, and received the return pass behind the defender.

This play, when practiced long enough and hard enough, helps to weld a team together and give it the confidence needed for winning.

Chapter 5
Defense

MISTAKE

Being faked out

Nothing feels so silly as being faked out in public. A good forward near the penalty box can often fake out the player who does not stay alert. This is usually done with a series of sidesteps and feint-steps. The forward gives the impression that he's about to receive a pass.

The defender (dark jersey) goes along with the fake and is thus taken out of the play, leaving his poor goalie on his own to defend against a charging halfback's shot.

CORRECTION

If you are the defender, you should watch legs, eyes, and bodies which give clues about the nature of the attack being aimed at you and your goal. By keeping your eye on the ball and on the legs of the attacker who has possession of the ball, you can often tell in an instant whether he is determined to shoot or pass. At this point, you must charge in and try to tackle the ball, letting the faker go his way.

MISTAKE

Square stance

Soccer is a game of balance and stance. If you are on the defensive and take a squared-off offensive position with one leg beside the other, you have given yourself a very shaky base from which to head off a determined offensive player. You won't be able to get off to a fast start from this position and the slightest contact with your body by your opponent could easily knock you out of the play. Moreover, if you're standing square and still, you can't move backwards quickly and your opponent can easily accelerate past you.

CORRECTION

Studying the greatest soccer players reveals that one foot should be behind the other for best results in most game situations. The body's weight should principally rest on that staunch back leg. This keeps the front leg free to make faster starts while that back leg provides a sturdy defense base from which to operate.

You should be poised on the balls of your feet, prepared to move in any direction quickly, always remembering to stay between your opponent and your own goal if possible.

MISTAKE

Sloppy sideline defense

As a defender it's a mistake not to exert every effort and use every skill you have to keep your opponent from leaving the sideline area with the ball and making it towards the "inside" or center of the field. Most of the big trouble in defensive soccer comes from the mid-field area where there's lots of room for enemy maneuvering and attack. When you have him near the sidelines that offender can't be nearly as offensive as when you let up and he gets through your defense.

54

CORRECTION

The trick is to keep moving as fast or agilely as you can and *to stay between the ball and the goal.* The best way to stop your attacker is by running him into an area *you* wish him to be in (sidelines, corner, back). You must therefore work to keep the initiative. Try to use your body and speed to attack your attacker and keep him near the least advantageous areas.

A good defender can take the initiative away from the offensive team by making that team do things it doesn't usually do. For example, a good defender can move an attacker into poor shooting angles, and cause him to use his weaker foot in many situations, giving himself an advantage.

MISTAKE

Unnecessary trip

If an offensive player has dribbled past you and you are giving chase from behind, don't reach in with your leg and try to get the ball. You will invariably trip your opponent, possibly injuring him. Almost as bad: Tripping is a "direct kick" penalty foul, meaning you are giving your opponent a free kick at your goal! (Note: Three of Coach Ed Kositzki's soccer teams that had made it into all-state tournaments *lost games by allowing penalty kicks for tripping!)*

CORRECTION

In order to make a fair tackle in soccer (As noted earlier a soccer tackle means trying to gain possession of the ball from your foe by using your feet.) you must first catch up with your opponent. When your legs are even with his you must then quickly pivot on the inside leg—the one closer to him. With the other leg you must try to make contact with the ball, retrieve it, and turn it back upfield towards the enemy goal. Not an easy task!

Tripping usually occurs because of over-eagerness or laziness. Generally you can run faster without the ball than your opponent can with it. This gives you the edge in catching up and making your tackle.

MISTAKE

Bunching up

Whether you're on the professional circuit or in a school game it's almost always wrong for *too many* defense players to try at the same time to repossess the ball from an attacker.

CORRECTION

No matter how badly the odds seem to be stacked against the attacker, "too many feet spoil the play." The crowding and confusion caused by three or more members of the same team trying to tackle a lone attacker often results in a successful attacker and an embarrassed gaggle of defenders.

MISTAKE

Poorly built wall

In close games, the dead ball situation, such as a direct free kick, often determines the outcome of a contest. Many times the game is lost by the defense setting up a wall improperly and giving a skillful striker a chance to curve his shot around the outermost man into the goal. The chances of this calamity occurring are increased when the wall is set up in such a way that the goalie can't see his attacker.

CORRECTION

The goalie should always be in charge of setting up the wall. It is, after all, designed to protect and aid him in his job of keeping that ball out of his net.

To keep that artful striker from curving his shot around the outermost man, it's a good practice to have the wall overlap the post by one player, as shown. (Our point of view for the overlap, of course, is from the ball, the kicker's-eye-view. But the goalie must use a certain amount of judgment from his position to set his overlap man in the right position.)

The primary rule is clear vision for the goalie. He must always be able to see the ball. The goalie should always be in the farther side of the nets.

61

Chapter 6
Offense

MISTAKE

Skip lunge time

Never lunge into a tackle, because it leaves you at your most vulnerable. Your opponent can go left or right, or pass to a teammate and leave you out of the play.

64

CORRECTION

It is wiser to *give ground*—that is hang back slightly—until your opponent, the forward, has kicked the ball slightly in front of himself/herself and the ball is not under his/her direct control.

This is the best time to make your move and steal the ball!

MISTAKE

Waiting and watching

A striker (white jersey) should never stay behind a defending fullback watching the ball and waiting for it to come his way. A good fullback or goalie will usually take the ball away from him or deflect it.

That goalie should not be waiting and watching that stiffly either!

CORRECTION

A good striker will try to stand behind and in the blind spot of a fullback until the pass or cross (a kick from the side-lines towards the center or penalty area) is made. At this point he runs in *front* of that defending fullback towards the ball. He tries to beat him to the ball for a kick or header shot at the goal.

67

MISTAKE

Soft shooting

In the excitement of getting within shooting range of the enemy goal, the new soccer player sometimes kicks wildly without picking out a target area. This often results in a soft, uncoordinated shot to the goalie who makes an easy save.

CORRECTION

Control is the name of the shooting game. You must be in control of the ball and be able to get your body's weight and power into your shot. You must learn to pick out a target, such as the corner just past the goalie. Your eyes should stay focused on the ball as you kick, and your kick should have good follow-through after you've made contact. You must also stay alert in case the ball comes back at you at an unpredictable angle.

MISTAKE

Improper throw-in

Every player at some time has to "throw-in" the ball from the sidelines after an out-of-bounds play. When throwing the ball back into the game the idea is to get it to the teammate in the best possible position to move the ball forward.

Letting your back (trailing) leg lift from the ground while you throw-in is the mark of an unskilled soccer player. That rear leg lifting during the throw-in sacrifices much of the body's throwing power and results in a weak toss that could easily end up in your opponent's control. A bad throw-in means giving up the ball without making your opponent fight for it, a step on the road to defeat.

CORRECTION

The body is a coiled spring when this maneuver is done properly. The trailing foot stays along the ground moving forward as the body's spring uncoils and the ball is catapulted forward.

Chapter 7
Goalkeeping

MISTAKE

Throwing to goalie

Helping a goalie warm up is crucial to his performance in a game. Teammates sometimes try to do this by throwing or rolling the ball to him. But in the long run, this kind of practice is useless.

74

CORRECTION

Almost all of the balls a goalie must handle come from the enemy's foot or head. His coordination must relate instantly to the kicked or headed ball. The kicker or header's distance should change during the warm-up, as should the speed of the kicks and their distances. These are called reaction drills, because the crucial element is the goalie's swift reaction time to the incoming ball.

MISTAKE

Not relying on reflexes

For the goalie soccer is a game of touch. Too often, in well-organized or even makeshift practice, the goalie's eyes are given more of a workout than his fingers and hands. The ball is thrust at him from close-up in some drills and he wheels away with it and kicks it. Sometimes, he misses the close-in thrust and bobbles the ball. This is usually the result of the eyes and hands working at a slightly different pace.

CORRECTION

(A goalie's hands must, literally, be quicker than the eye.) Goalkeeping is in large part an art of instantaneous *feelings* and reactions. "There is no time to 'think,'" says Coach Ed Kositzki. "It's all reflexes."

In practice, the goalie must spend some of his time having the ball fed to him while his eyes are momentarily shut! This helps evolve confidence in his hands

and develops the "feel" in his fingers.

A good drill has a player or series of players thrust the ball at the goalie from behind. Let the fingers do the seeing!

Once a goalie develops the ability to "see" with those fingers, he/she is on the way to superior performance. Practicing finger reaction leads to proper game action.

MISTAKE

Motionless goalie

On a penalty shot the goalie should never present a static, unmoving target, anticipating the shot. The reflexes required for goaltending can't work efficiently when a body is at rest. Split seconds lost in getting started can be deadly.

CORRECTION

Soccer goalies operate best using a little movement, with legs apart at shoulder-width, knees bent and flexing, arms extended and gently moving. The movement, aside from charging up the goalie's reflexes for instant release, serves to distract the attacker.

The extended arms and coiled-spring knees give the goalie the best chance of diving left, or right to the low corners, or leaping straight up in a "push-off" for a save, to cover those high corners.

If you're leaping to the left, push off with your left leg. If you go right, the right leg does the pushing.

MISTAKE

Standing on the goal line

When the goalie stands on the goal line he gives the kicker much too much of the net as a target. From the goal line position it's almost impossible to dive into either corner for a save.

CORRECTION

A goalie should station himself several feet in front of the goal line. This reduces advantageous angles for the kicker and permits the goalie a fighting chance at a dive to one side or the other for a save.

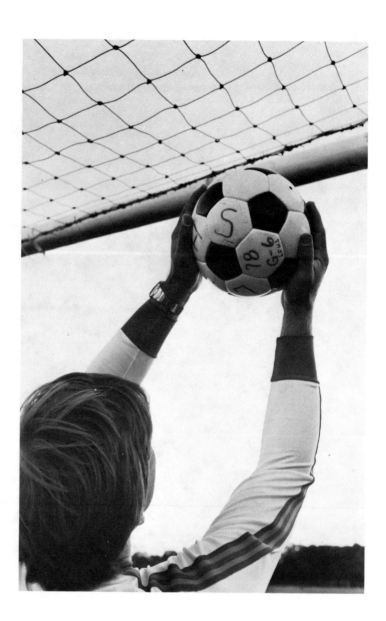

MISTAKE

Thumbless grip

Would-be goalies generally have good basic reflexes, but get into bad saving habits that are hard to unlearn.

The foremost of these is depending on an instant clasp of the hands on the fleeting ball for a save. The reflexive motion is to keep the hands in the "applause" position the instant the ball is touched.

This thumbless grip works fine on easy shots at the goal, but when the hard, curving, wet-ball shots come in, not setting up a trifle differently becomes a costly liability to the team.

CORRECTION

The trick is quite simple. Use those thumbs—whose agility separates us from the other primates—and use them to form a back-up wall behind the eight fingers commonly used in the "applause" position.

Those two back-up thumbs not only save lots of goals, but when you learn to keep them well back and out, your chances of getting hit on the thumb by the ball head-on are minimized.

MISTAKE

Throwing error

The goalie makes a fine save out in front of the net. Then without wasting a move, he hurls the ball back in the direction from which it came, often giving the attacker, who can possibly intercept, another shot at him!

CORRECTION

If you're the goalie and have to or want to make a quick throw after a save, throw the ball in the opposite direction from which it came—toward your own teammates of course.

MISTAKE

Catch-as-catch-can

To catch-as-catch-can a soccer ball is not good enough for an aspiring goalie. Of course in a desperation move, any successful catch is OK, but the groundwork of good catching for a goalie involves using much more than the hands.

The hands-alone goalie is not living up to his full potential as the team's last defender against an enemy goal. A hard shot can easily slip through the fingers and, most embarrassing, through legs that are too far apart.

CORRECTION

Just as in the high catch at the net's entrance, the goalie making a ground catch must form a good web with his thumbs and index fingers. This provides an instant improvement over a kind of slap-catch in which the hands close on the ball in a quick slap. The legs should be just far enough apart *not to permit a soccer ball to roll through.* The waist should be supple and rocking slightly in anticipation of an attacking shot. The body must be thought of as the back-up shield for the palms and thumbs. It often serves just that function.

Most good goalies yell, "Got it!" as a shot comes their way. This gives the rest of the defending line a chance to get ready for the next move instantly.

Old-time goalies used to sink to one knee to help make a save. This costs time and energy in the moment after the save, because the goalie has to use valuable time, and often space, to get up and throw or kick.

If the ball can't be caught, it should be punched or otherwise deflected.

MISTAKE

Poor knee reading

A goalie who must defend against a penalty shot and decides to play slightly left or right in front of the goal has a 50 percent chance of being right. This isn't good enough for winning soccer! He/she must learn to read the signs of the attacking striker. Ignoring these signs can cost lots of goals.

A right-footed kicker, for example, whose knee turns outward at the moment he kicks most often kicks the ball to his right. The goalie who can't read this sign quickly won't be moving to his left and won't get the crucial jump on the ball that separates the good goalie from the ordinary ones.

CORRECTION

The goalie who instantly perceives the kicker turning that knee inward can count on the ball going to the striker's left. The wise goalie therefore moves right in anticipation and makes a good save!

The name of the game, of course, is anticipation. Goalies must learn to read the signs instantaneously.

MISTAKE

Diving in the wrong direction

If you're the goalie and the ball is coming in fast and to your right you know you have to dive. If you take off on any foot that happens to be supporting your body, you only have a 50 percent chance of doing the right thing!

90

CORRECTION

When you dive to the right you should take off on your right foot.

When you dive to the left you should take off on your left foot.

The two- or three-step run to this leap should give you the momentum you need to get to the ball.

Chapter 8
Sportsmanship

MISTAKE

Official madness

The soccer referee and his linespeople are human. The player who constantly disputes their calls and decisions can't help but antagonize even the fairest-minded official. In a really tight judgment call the referee's honest opinion—even what he actually sees—can easily be influenced by the past behavior of a troublesome, heckling player. This could end up costing a goal or a game plus the scorn of teammates who should be friends.

94

CORRECTION

It should be understood from long before game time that the referee's word is law. It is natural to be disappointed at a call that works against you but this disappointment is something that a serious soccer player must learn to accept rather than use as a way of getting even with "that blind official."

Learn to smile, to be polite, to be a sportsperson on the field. The soccer field is much smaller than the outside world, but the rules are much the same. If you are good, fair, and pleasant to people, they will treat you the same way.

Remember, soccer is a sport, not all-out war!